Funtastic Math

Problem Solving and Logic

by Martin Lee and Marcia Miller

SCHOLASTIC
PROFESSIONAL BOOKS

New York ✳ Toronto ✳ London ✳ Auckland ✳ Sydney

For Josh and David

A special thanks to Melanie Pace Kinslow and her 1997–1998
fifth-grade class at Gullett Elementary School

Edited by Sarah Glasscock

Cover design by Jaime Lucero

Interior design by Ellen Matlach Hassell
for Boultinghouse & Boultinghouse, Inc.

Interior illustrations by Ellen Joy Sasaki and Manuel Rivera

ISBN 0-590-37368-4

Contents

(continued on the next page)

✳ Activity includes a student reproducible.

LOGIC

✳ Activity includes a student reproducible.

Introduction

With this book of activities, part of a six-book mathematics series, we hope to make teaching and understanding problem solving and logic fun, creative, and exciting.

⟳➤ An Overview of the Book

Table of Contents

The table of contents features the activity names and page numbers, as well as stars to mark student reproducibles.

Teaching Pages

Everything you need to know is on the teaching page, but you also have the option of tailoring the activities to meet the students' individual needs and to address the wide variety of skills displayed in your classroom.

Learning Logo

A logo indicating whether problem solving or logic is the focus of the activity appears at the top of the page.

Learning Objective

The objective clearly states the primary aim of the activity.

Grouping

This states whether the whole class, individual students, pairs, or cooperative groups should perform the task. If an activity lends itself to more than one grouping, the choices are indicated. Again, if you feel that another grouping is more appropriate to your classroom, feel free to alter the activity accordingly.

Materials

To cut your preparation time, all materials necessary for the main activity (including student reproducible) and its extension are listed. Most of the materials are probably already in your classroom. If an activity has a student reproducible with it, the page number of the reproducible is listed here.

Advance Preparation

A few activities require some minimal advance preparation on your part. All the directions you need are given here. You may also let students take over some or all of the preparation.

Directions

The directions usually begin with suggestions on how to introduce the activity, including any terms and/or formulas. Step-by-step details on how to do the activity follow. When pertinent, specific strategies that might help students in solving problems are suggested.

Taking It Farther

This section on the teaching page offers suggestions on how you can extend and enrich the activity. Students who require extra help and those who need a challenge will both benefit when you move the activity to a different level.

Assessing Skills

The key questions and/or common errors pointed out in this section will help alert you to students' progress. (In fact, you may want to jot down more questions on the page.) Use the information you gather about students here in conjunction with the teacher assessment form that appears on page 63 of the book.

Answers

When answers are called for, they appear at the bottom of the teaching page. If the answer is in the form of a drawing or diagram, it will appear on page 64, and you are advised of that at the bottom of the teaching page.

Student Reproducibles

About one-third of the activities have a companion student reproducible page for you to duplicate and distribute. These activities are marked with a star in the table of contents.

Do I Have Problems!

These pages are filled with fun and challenging Problems of the Day that you may write on the board or post on the bulletin board. The answers appear in brackets at the end of each problem.

Assessment

Student Self-Evaluation Form

At the end of the activity, hand out these forms for students to complete. Emphasize that their responses are for themselves as well as you. Evaluating their own performances will help students clarify their own thinking and understand more about their reasoning.

Teacher Assessment Form and Scoring Rubric

The sign of a student's success with an activity is more than a correct answer. As the NCTM stresses, problem solving, communication, reasoning, and connections are equally important in the mathematical process. How a student arrives at the answer—the strategies she or he uses or discards, for instance—can be as important as the answer itself. This assessment form and scoring rubric will help you determine the full range of students' mastery of skills.

National Council of Teachers of Mathematics Standards

The activities in this book, and the rest of the series, have been written with the National Council of Teachers of Mathematics (NCTM) Standards in mind. The first four standards—Mathematics as Problem Solving, Mathematics as Communication, Mathematics as Reasoning, and Mathematical Connections—form the philosophical underpinning of the activities.

Standard 1 Mathematics as Problem Solving
The open-ended structure of the activities, and their extension, builds and strengthens students' problem-solving skills.

Standard 2 Mathematics as Communication
Class discussion at the beginning and ending of the activities is an integral part of these activities.

Additionally, communication is fostered when students work in pairs or cooperative groups and when individuals share and compare work.

Standard 3 Mathematics as Reasoning
Communicating their processes in working these activities gives students the opportunity to understand and appreciate their own thinking.

Standard 4 Mathematical Connections
A variety of situations has been incorporated into the activities to give students a broad base on which to apply mathematics. Topics range from real-life experiences (historical and contemporary) to the whimsical and fantastic, so students can expand their mathematical thinking to include other subject areas.

More specifically, the activities in this book address the following NCTM Standards.

Grades K–4:

Standard 1: Mathematics as Problem Solving
* Use problem-solving approaches to investigate and understand mathematical content.
* Formulate problems from everyday and mathematical situations.
* Develop and apply strategies to solve a wide variety of problems.
* Verify and interpret results with respect to the original problem.
* Acquire confidence in using mathematics meaningfully.

Standard 3: Mathematics as Reasoning
* Draw logical conclusions about mathematics.
* Use models, known facts, properties, and relationships to explain their thinking.
* Justify their answers and solution processes.
* Use patterns and relationships to analyze mathematical situations.
* Believe that mathematics makes sense.

Grades 5–8:

Standard 1: Mathematics as Problem Solving
* Use problem-solving approaches to investigate and understand mathematical content.
* Formulate problems from situations within and outside mathematics.
* Develop and apply a variety of strategies to solve problems, with emphasis on multistep and nonroutine problems.
* Verify and interpret results with respect to the original problem situation.
* Generalize solutions and strategies to new problem situations.
* Acquire confidence in using mathematics meaningfully.

Standard 3: Mathematics as Reasoning
* Recognize and apply deductive and inductive reasoning.
* Understand and apply reasoning processes, with special attention to spatial reasoning and reasoning with proportions and graphs.
* Make and evaluate mathematical conjectures and arguments.
* Validate their own thinking.
* Appreciate the pervasive use and power of reasoning as part of mathematics.

What, No Numbers?

The real-life math problems on these pages require answers, yet they have no numbers!

➤ Directions

1. Present the following problem: *Julio used his savings to buy a bike. The total amount he paid included sales tax. How much of his savings remained after the purchase?*

2. Ask students which operation they would use for each step in the solution and what they would add, subtract, multiply, or divide.

3. Guide students to see that to solve this problem, first they add the amount of the sales tax to the price of the bike, then subtract that sum from the amount of savings. Point out that if the sales tax were given as a percent, they would need to divide to express the percent as a decimal or fraction and then multiply to find that percent of the price of the bike.

4. Suggest to students that to better understand the problem, they can fill in sensible amounts for the unstated numbers. For instance, they might choose $200 for the bike, 5% for the sales tax, and $500 for the amount of savings.

5. Duplicate the *What, No Numbers?* reproducible for each individual or pair. Have students complete the page on their own or with partners. Encourage them to think of a variety of solution plans.

★ Taking It Farther

Ask students to work in pairs. One creates a multistep problem with no numbers. The other gives the steps in the solution. Or one student provides only numerical data, and the other student writes a sensible problem using that data.

✓ Assessing Skills

✳ Do students come up with more than one way to solve a problem?

✳ Can they explain their strategies and answers?

LEARNING OBJECTIVE

Students choose combinations of operations to solve problems for which no numbers are provided.

GROUPING

Individual or pairs

MATERIALS

✳ *What, No Numbers?* reproducible (p. 9)

ANSWERS

1. Multiply the cost of an individual ticket by the number of tickets in the booklet; subtract what Max paid from that product.

2. Divide the miles Inez ran by the number of hours she ran.

3. Subtract the "before" odometer reading from the "after" reading; divide that result by the number of gallons used.

4. Possible answer: divide the price of each box by its weight—the smaller quotient indicates the better buy.

5. Multiply the profit per paper by the number of papers Li delivers (in a day or week); divide by the number of hours she works (in a day or week).

6. Possible answer: Double the mean weight; subtract the difference in their weights from that sum; divide by 2 to find Eva's weight; add the difference to find Vera's weight.

What, No Numbers?

The problems below have no numbers. Decide how you would solve each one. Tell what you would add, subtract, multiply, or divide to find the answer. If it helps you, fill in reasonable numbers.

1. Max saved some money by buying a book of movie passes rather than individual tickets. How can he figure out how much money he saved?

_____

_____

2. Inez knows the number of miles she ran last week. She knows how many hours she ran. How can she figure out her rate of speed in miles per hour?

_____

_____

3. Ed knows his car's odometer readings (in miles) before and after a trip. He knows the number of gallons of gasoline he used. How can he figure out the number of miles-per-gallon his car got on the trip?

_____

4. Pat knows the weight and price of two different-size boxes of dry cat food. How can he figure out which of the two is the better buy?

_____

_____

5. Li has a paper route. She delivers a certain number of papers every day. For each paper she delivers, she makes the same amount of money. How can she figure out her hourly wage?

_____

_____

6. Vera weighs more than Eva. You know how much more. You know the mean weight of the two. How can you figure out how much each weighs?

_____

_____

estimating * logical reasoning * organizing * visual

Laces

Some problems or tasks may appear overwhelming at first. But once students break them down into smaller, manageable parts, they can find the answers.

Directions

1. Present the following problem: *About how many feet—the measurement, not the part of the body—of shoelaces are in our school right now?*

2. Invite students to make guesses. Then challenge groups to come up with a series of steps they can use to make a closer approximation of the answer. Groups should record their plans.

3. Emphasize that many approaches are possible and that whatever method groups use, they should be sure that each member participates in a meaningful way.

4. Guide students to record all data as they go.

5. If students are stuck initially, point out that one way to start is to measure the length of a few shoelaces to come up with a typical length to use in the investigation. One approach students can use is to estimate the total shoelace length of their own group or class.

6. Have groups present and discuss their answers and describe their strategies.

7. Compare final estimates with initial guesses.

Taking It Farther

Challenge students to plan a way to estimate the number of pounds of math textbooks in the school, the area of all the windows in the building, the total wattage of all the lights, the number of pieces of pasta the cafeteria uses on macaroni and cheese day, or anything else of interest to them.

Assessing Skills

* Do students have a workable plan for solving the problem?
* Do their estimates make sense?
* Does their presentation fully explain what they did and how they did it?

LEARNING OBJECTIVE

Students do an investigation in which they use small steps to solve a multistep problem.

GROUPING

Cooperative groups

MATERIALS

* ruler or tape measure
* calculator (optional)

The Typical American President

George Washington was from Virginia. When he was inaugurated in 1789, he was 57 years old. In what ways was the first president a typical president?

⟶ Directions

1. Tell students that they are going to figure out a way to characterize the typical American chief executive by gathering and analyzing personal data about all the presidents.

2. Brainstorm with students to list easily obtainable characteristics by which presidents can be compared and contrasted. Topics may include state of birth, age at inauguration, marital status, career prior to entering politics, length of term, and so on. For instance, George Washington studied math and surveying and had a career in the military. He married Martha Custis in 1759. Encourage groups to adjust and add to any list the class creates.

3. Help students find sources such as almanacs for locating the data they need. Emphasize the usefulness of recording data in an organized way, such as in a table.

4. Discuss ways to analyze the data, such as finding averages. Talk about which measures of central tendency—mean, median, or mode—are most useful in describing typical characteristics.

5. Make sure all group members share in researching, recording, and analyzing.

6. Have groups present their findings.

☆ Taking It Farther

Let students summarize the groups' findings. Ask who comes closer to the class's idea of the typical president, George Washington or the current occupant of the White House.

✔ Assessing Skills

✳ Do students identify data they can compare for all or most presidents?

✳ Do they use statistics effectively to analyze their data?

✳ Do groups come up with unique characteristics to compare or ways to analyze their data?

LEARNING OBJECTIVE

Students examine data about American presidents to come up with specific characteristics that describe "the typical president."

GROUPING

Cooperative groups

MATERIALS

✳ almanac or other sources of information about U.S. presidents

✳ calculator (optional)

Pets Step Up

Correctly interpreting information in store flyers, catalogs, and ads is a real-life skill students need to become smarter shoppers.

⟶ Directions

1. Review with students the kinds of information usually provided in ads for consumer products. Discuss the different ways that products are discounted and how that information may be presented.

2. Duplicate a copy of the *Pets Step Up* reproducible for each pair.

3. Instruct partners to answer the questions on the reproducible. Point out that in some cases they'll need to calculate, while in others it may make better sense to use their estimating skills. Encourage students to use the most reasonable calculation method: calculator, paper and pencil, or mental math.

4. Discuss students' answers. If necessary, guide them to explain the strategies they used.

☆ Taking It Farther

Invite students to formulate additional questions based on the information in the ad. Or you might have them create their own humorous ads, along with questions, for an interactive bulletin board.

✔ Assessing Skills

✳ Do students demonstrate an ability to interpret data presented in an ad and show that they can find sale prices given information about discounts?

✳ Do they choose the most sensible computational method?

✳ Do students always find exact answers, or do they make estimates when that approach is reasonable and sufficient?

LEARNING OBJECTIVE

Students use information from an advertisement to solve problems involving discounts. They decide whether to find an exact answer or make an estimate.

GROUPING

Pairs

MATERIALS

✳ *Pets Step Up* reproducible (p. 13)

✳ calculator (optional)

ANSWERS

1. $30.50
2. yes
3. *20 Hours of Sleep—Is That Enough?*
4. *How to Get More and Better Meals, Total Turtle Training*
5. *Getting Away with Scratching*

Pets Step Up

Educated pets make the best customers. So fur is flying at Claws and Paws Pet Shop because all pet self-help books and tapes are on sale.

Help your pet use the information from the ad to answer the questions.

BIG BOOK AND VIDEO SALE!

Videos	Books
Getting Away with Scratching was $29.95; now $5 off	**Life On a Leash:** **Tips and Strategies** $4.50 off original price of $30
Power Poodles originally $22; now $2.50 off	**How to Get More and Better Meals** was $14.95; now $5 off with another purchase
Total Turtle Training $\frac{1}{2}$ off original price of $15.99	**20 Hours of Sleep—Is That Enough?** $\frac{1}{4}$ off original price of $18.88

ALL OUR LOW PRICES INCLUDE SALES TAX!

1. You have a $50 bill. What is your change if you buy the *Power Poodles* video?

_____

2. You have $40. Can you buy *Total Turtle Training* and *Life on a Leash: Tips and Strategies*? If not, how much more money would you need to borrow from your pet?

_____

3. Your pet had you spend $14.16. Which book or video did you buy?

_____

4. You have $20 to spend. Order two items that will cost less than that in all.

_____

5. You spent just under $75 on three of the same book or video. Which one did you buy?

_____

Car for Rent

Rooting through the assortment of rental car options can cause anyone's engine to overheat!

➤ Directions

1. Tell students that they will plan a round-trip using one of several car rental plans. Duplicate the *Car for Rent* reproducible for each student or pair. Go over each rental plan with students. To help them understand the plans, you might work through the cost of one or more imaginary trips using each plan. For instance, find and compare costs of a 3-day trip of 1,000 miles, then a 7-day trip of 3,000 miles.

2. Make road atlases available. Have students work in pairs or small groups so that they can help one another read the atlas.

3. Direct students to choose destinations at least several hundred miles from their homes. Discuss all factors that will affect the number of days they'll need the car, such as the distance they're likely to drive in a day and the time they'll spend eating, sleeping, and sightseeing on their trips. As needed, review the distance formula, $d = rt$.

4. Have students complete the page and then share their findings. Ask them how to select the best plan for the different types of trips—a trip that's close to home, a trip of great distance or duration, or one that involves a drop-off at a different location.

⭐ Taking It Farther

Challenge students to research rental plans at actual car agencies. They can find the plan that would work best for their proposed trip.

✔ Assessing Skills

✳ Have students accurately determined the length of the trip and estimated the time it would take?

✳ Have they applied each plan correctly to obtain the correct costs?

LEARNING OBJECTIVE

Students solve a real-life problem by using pricing information, a road atlas, and common sense.

GROUPING

Pairs or small groups

MATERIALS

✳ *Car for Rent* reproducible (p. 15)

✳ road atlas for North America (approximately 1 for every 2–3 students)

✳ calculator (optional)

Car for Rent

Here's your chance to see the U.S.A.— without leaving your classroom!

The following car rental plans are from Take Off Rent-a-Car.

PLAN A	**PLAN B**	**PLAN C**
$32.95 per day	$27.95 per day	$45 per day
500 free miles	no free miles	1,500 free miles
then $0.20 a mile	$0.25 a mile	then $0.30 a mile

1. Choose a North American destination you'd like to visit. How about the Statue of Liberty, Big Bend National Park, Monument Valley, or the Everglades? Plot a route to the spot you pick. Map out and record the route and estimate the driving distance.

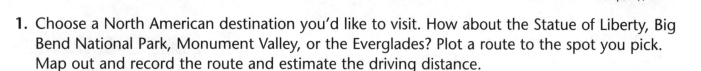

_____

_____

_____

2. Figure out how long the entire round-trip would take. Remember: You can't drive all day long, and you need to sleep, eat, get gas, and spend some time at the place you're visiting. And don't forget those speed limits!

_____

_____

_____

_____

3. Determine the cost of the car rental for your entire round-trip, using each plan. Which plan makes the most sense for you? Why?

_____

_____

_____

_____

Car Wash

People commonly need to estimate how long everyday activities take. For instance, washing a car. How long *does* it take to wash a car?

⚙→ Directions

1. Ask students to make a quick estimate of how long they think it takes to wash a car. Record the responses on the board.

2. Tell students that their job is to analyze the task of washing a car, from start to finish, so they can present a more accurate estimate. Have them assume that the dirty vehicle is already in a driveway, that a hose and a water source are at hand, and that towels, rags, soap, and all other materials they'll need are in the garage or the house. They can decide whether to do the washing alone or work with a partner.

3. Have students brainstorm to break down the car-washing process into its discrete parts and then list these tasks in a sensible order. Emphasize that the more precisely they break down the job, the closer they'll come to making an accurate estimate of the time it will take to complete it.

4. As needed, review computing with time values.

5. Allow time for students to share and discuss their estimates with classmates. Have them compare their detailed estimates with their initial guesses and identify reasons for any differences. Encourage them to talk about why classmates' estimates vary.

✪ Taking It Farther

Have students use their classmates' estimates to find the range of car-washing times and the mean time. If possible, invite a volunteer actually to wash a car, keeping track of the time all parts of the job take.

✔ Assessing Skills

✳ Have students carefully broken down the car-washing task into its many parts to make a more accurate estimate of the total time the job will take?

✳ Are their estimates reasonable? If not, can they make sensible adjustments?

LEARNING OBJECTIVE

Students use logic, common sense, and estimating skills to predict how long a task will take.

GROUPING

Individual or pairs

MATERIALS

None

On the Beaten Path

Sometimes drawing a picture or diagram is the best way to solve a problem. It's certainly a good strategy to use to solve the problem presented below.

☼➔ Directions

1. Have students record the key data as you read aloud the following problem:

    In MacPherson State Park, a guided nature trail leads from the visitor center to the falls. It's $\frac{1}{3}$ mile from the visitor center to the giant oak and another $\frac{3}{4}$ mile to the abandoned mine. It's half a mile from there to the stream. From the stream it's another $\frac{3}{8}$ mile to the falls. Hikers must stay on the trail at all times. Luke started back from the falls at the same time Lisa started out from the parking lot. Each walked 1 mile and stopped. Who was closer to the mine at that point? Who was closer to the parking lot? [Lisa, by $\frac{1}{24}$ mile; Luke, by $\frac{1}{24}$ mile]

2. Guide students to draw and label a diagram of the trail to solve this problem. As needed, review finding common denominators and renaming fractions. Also reread the problem as necessary.

3. Ask volunteers to draw on the board or overhead projector the diagrams they made and then explain how they obtained the answers. Invite students who used other methods to explain their approaches.

4. Make up or invite students to create other problems of this type. You might consider including directionality—3 miles south, then 4.5 miles west, and so on.

✪ Taking It Farther

Challenge students to use road atlases to make up problems much like the nature trail problem but that use real information.

✓ Assessing Skills

* Have students accurately recorded the information you presented?
* Do their diagrams show the information correctly?
* Can students explain how they got their answers to the problem?

LEARNING OBJECTIVE

Students use listening skills to record the information in a problem. They draw a diagram to solve the problem.

GROUPING

Individual

MATERIALS

* paper and pencil
* road atlas for North America (optional)
* overhead projector (optional)

Following Directions

How good are students at following directions, even straightforward ones? Try this activity to find out. The results might surprise you.

⟲→ Directions

1. Tell students that their challenge in this activity is to follow simple but exact instructions to draw a picture within a frame. Emphasize that the instructions contain specific geometric language and must be followed precisely.

2. Duplicate the two *Following Directions* reproducibles and give a set to each student.

3. Alternatively, you may want students to work in pairs; one reads the instructions, the other draws the picture. Or you might choose to read the instructions aloud.

4. Have students post their drawings to compare and discuss them.

5. Invite students to make up their own sets of instructions for classmates to follow to the letter, with the answers drawn on the back. They can post these on the bulletin board. Other students can work on these when time permits.

★ Taking It Farther

Direct students to write out specific sets of instructions for getting from one place (such as school) to another in the neighborhood—but without identifying the destination. Challenge others to follow the directions carefully to identify the destination.

✓ Assessing Skills

✻ How accurately have students followed the instructions?

✻ Do students understand where (if anywhere) they fell short and how to fix it?

✻ Have students who have made up their own sets of directions answered them correctly?

LEARNING OBJECTIVE

Students follow specific instructions to draw a picture.

GROUPING

Individual or pairs

MATERIALS

✻ *Following Directions* reproducibles (pp. 19–20)

✻ metric ruler calibrated in millimeters

✻ pennies

✻ colored markers or pencils

ANSWERS

See page 64.

Following Directions

Following these directions will definitely make you feel like you've been framed!
But you'll have created a work of art you may really want to frame.

Carefully follow these instructions, in order, to draw a picture within the frame. You'll need a metric ruler.

1. From point X, draw a 6-cm line segment toward the center of the frame.

2. Where the segment ends, draw a circle the size of a penny. Make the segment end at the top of this circle.

3. Within the circle, write the customary unit of length you would use to give the distance between two state capitals.

4. From the bottom of the circle, draw a line segment 40 mm long toward the right edge of the frame, parallel to the bottom edge.

5. At the end of this segment, draw a small square. Write your age in months and days to the right of the square.

6. From the upper right corner of the square, draw a line segment to the midpoint shown at the top edge of the frame. Label that point Y.

7. From point Y, draw a line segment that ends about 0.3 dm from the bottom left corner of the frame. Label the end of this segment Z.

8. Using point Z as the upper left corner, draw a rectangle with a base of 75 mm and a height of 15 mm. Print your name inside it.

9. Draw a line segment to connect the bottom of the circle to the top of the rectangle at a point $\frac{2}{3}$ of the way from point Z.

10. Measure the length of this segment to the nearest centimeter. Write the measurement to the right of the segment.

Following Directions

Problem Solving and Logic Scholastic Professional Books

Behind the Lines

Can students look at a line graph that has no title, no labels, and no scale, and come up with an interpretation for what it shows?

➔ Directions

1. On the board or overhead projector, draw a line graph on an 8 × 8 grid without writing a title, labeling axes, or numbering the vertical and horizontal scales. Make a line graph that begins level and gradually rises by using (1, 2), (2, 2), (3, 2), (4, 3), (5, 4), (6, 4), and (7, 5) as coordinates.

2. Remind students that a line graph shows change over time. Ask them to suggest an everyday situation that fits the graph. For instance, someone might say the graph shows that a student's test scores rose once he or she began to study. Or they might say it shows that as a runner got in better shape, he or she began to run longer distances. Invite students to describe as many situations as they can.

3. You may want to repeat the process, this time using a graph with an entirely different shape, such as one that rises steeply and then drops off dramatically.

4. Then invite students to make up some line graphs of their own that represent everyday situations. Have them place their "incomplete" graphs on a bulletin board. On the back, they can describe what their graph shows.

5. Challenge students to place self-stick notes beneath the graphs to suggest situations each graph might show. As a class, discuss the reasonableness of these responses. Finally, compare the actual purposes of the graphs with the guesses.

⭐ Taking It Farther

Challenge students to add untitled circle graphs to the bulletin board.

✔ Assessing Skills

✴ Do students understand the kinds of information a line graph shows?

✴ Can they predict what a line graph shows when it's missing all numerical data, labels, and its title?

✴ Can students draw a line graph that shows the situation they intend it to show?

LEARNING OBJECTIVE

Students examine line graphs without titles and numbers and predict what each might represent.

GROUPING

Individual

MATERIALS

✴ graph paper
✴ self-stick notes
✴ overhead projector (optional)

Mapmaker, Mapmaker

On a political map, regions that share borders often have different colors. Mathematicians have proved that no map needs more than four colors.

Directions

1. Draw the three "maps" in step 2 on the board. Leave out the numbers. Tell students that regions sharing a border must have different colors. As needed, discuss and demonstrate what sharing a border means. Guide students to understand that regions that touch at only one point can have the same color. The Four Corners of the United States where Utah, Arizona, New Mexico, and Colorado join is an example; Utah and New Mexico or Arizona and Colorado could both be the same color. You may wish to have a globe or world atlas available for reference.

2. Then have students copy the maps below. Ask students to figure out the minimum number of colors needed to color each one. Allow time to go over their answers.

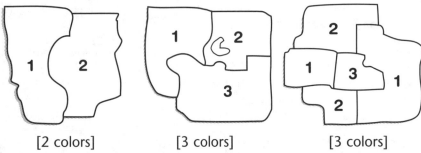

[2 colors]   [3 colors]   [3 colors]

3. Make a copy of the *Mapmaker, Mapmaker* reproducible for each student. Have them complete the page on their own.

4. Invite students to post their completed maps on the bulletin board.

☆ Taking It Farther

Challenge students to create three of their own maps—one that needs two colors, one that needs three, and one that needs four. Compile the uncolored maps in a folder. Invite students to color the maps as indicated.

✔ Assessing Skills

✳ Can students color the maps according to the directions?

✳ What generalizations can they make about the number of different colors a map needs?

LEARNING OBJECTIVE

Students color maps using only a given number of colors.

GROUPING

Individual

MATERIALS

✳ colored chalk
✳ assorted colored pencils
✳ *Mapmaker, Mapmaker* reproducible (p. 23)
✳ globe or world atlas (optional)

ANSWERS

See page 64.

Mapmaker, Mapmaker

Red, yellow, orange, blue, purple—which four colors
would you use to color a map of the world?

Color the maps using only the given number of colors.

1. Use 3 colors.

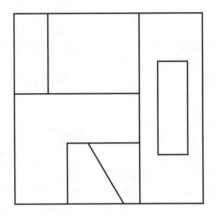

2. Use 4 colors.

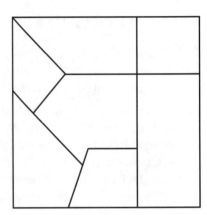

3. Color this map
using 4 colors.

Room Enough?

According to the 1997 edition of *The Guinness Book of Records*, as of 1993, Christopher Weide of Jacksonville, Florida, had collected 6,510 soda bottles.

☼➔ Directions

1. Tell students the fact about Mr. Weide's soda bottle collection. Then ask the class to imagine that the school principal has volunteered to use your classroom as the storage area for the collection.

2. Other than grouping students or forming pairs, provide no help with this task. You may, however, suggest that boxing the bottles for storage makes good sense. Allow enough time for groups to make measurements and do calculations. Encourage them to discuss the problem fully and decide on an organized plan before beginning the task. Remind groups that all members must participate in a meaningful way.

3. When groups present their results, have them describe their solution methods. Invite discussion of answers, strategies, and methods. Discuss which methods led to the most accurate answer and the quickest answer. Discuss which methods were the most creative.

✪ Taking It Farther

Challenge students to figure out how many basketballs (or tennis balls) their classroom can hold.

✔ Assessing Skills

✷ Do students find a reasonable answer for the question? Can they explain how they did it?

✷ Do they use proportional reasoning to find their answers efficiently?

✷ Can they apply what they've learned in this activity to another situation requiring visual/spatial estimation?

LEARNING OBJECTIVE

Students use spatial sense, critical thinking, and estimation to predict how much space is needed to hold a quantity of items.

GROUPING

Pairs or cooperative groups

MATERIALS

✷ measuring tools for length

✷ empty soda bottles of various sizes

✷ calculators (optional)

Piece of the Pie

If nobody cares about the size of the pieces, it will take fewer cuts than students think to slice a pizza.

⟳ Directions

1. Say that a student named Roland claims he can divide a round pizza for 11 friends by making only 4 straight cuts. Ask students to figure out if this can be true. Remind them that the pieces need not be the same size.

2. Point out that although using trial and error, a big circle, and a straightedge is one way of proving Roland right or wrong, another way is to find and extend a pattern. Ask students to make and complete a table showing the greatest number of pieces that can be formed by 0 cuts, 1 cut, 2 cuts, 3 cuts, and so on. Until they recognize the pattern, students can make drawings to help them fill in the table. You might have volunteers make drawings on the board or overhead projector for the greatest number of pieces formed by 1, 2, and 3 straight cuts.

3. Have students discuss the pattern that emerges for the greatest number of pieces per number of cuts. [The difference between the greatest number of pieces formed with each successive cut increases by 1: 0 cuts = 1 piece; 1 cut = 2 pieces; 2 cuts = 4 pieces; 3 cuts = 7 pieces; 4 cuts = 11 pieces; 5 cuts = 16 pieces; 6 cuts = 22 pieces; for instance, 2 – 1 = 1, 4 – 2 = 2, 7 – 4 = 3, 11 – 7 = 4, and so on.]

4. Ask students to draw large circles on sheets of paper and to try to draw all the different ways of making pieces with 4 cuts, 5 cuts, and 6 cuts. But first, guide them to come up with this rule of thumb they can apply when making the cuts: the more intersections there are, the more pieces there will be.

☆ Taking It Farther

Ask students to figure out the fewest number of straight cuts needed to divide a pizza for a not-too-hungry class of 27. [7 cuts = 29 pieces]

✔ Assessing Skills

✳ Do students discover the pattern for the maximum number of pieces formed by straight cuts? Can they apply this understanding to solve problems about a greater numbers of cuts?

✳ Are students able to draw all different ways to make pieces using 3, 4, 5, and 6 cuts?

LEARNING OBJECTIVE

Students figure out and extend a pattern. They apply their visual reasoning skills to explore the pattern.

GROUPING

Pairs

MATERIALS

✳ paper and pencils
✳ straightedge
✳ compass (optional)
✳ overhead projector (optional)

ANSWERS

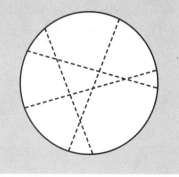

Think Again!

Satchel Paige, the legendary pitcher, said another player was so fast, he could turn out the light by his bedroom door and be in bed before the room was dark!

⟶ Directions

1. Share Satchel Paige's claim with students. Challenge them to explain why the story may not be as far-fetched as it seems. If students don't suggest it, point out that the player could have turned out the light during the daytime!

2. Guide students to understand that although some problems are created purposely to mislead, problem solvers can stay ahead of them by trying to avoid mistaken inferences. Present the following problem as an example: *Two coins total 30¢. One is not a nickel. What are the coins?* Guide students to recognize that the solution—a quarter and a nickel (the other coin is the nickel) becomes clear once you change the way you look at it. Suggest that students think to themselves, "What exactly does this problem say? What does it *not* say?"

3. Duplicate and distribute the *Think Again!* reproducible to each student or pair.

4. You may want to help students who struggle with the first problem on the reproducible by pointing out that they needn't assume that the lines must stay within the array. For the second and third problems, both classic brain teasers, point out that several answers are possible. Accept any responses students can justify.

☆ Taking It Farther

Challenge students to collect and publish a variety of similar math brain teasers for schoolmates and families. They can interview friends or family members, or do research in the library and on the Internet.

✓ Assessing Skills

✳ Are students able to identify hidden assumptions?

✳ Do they arrive at reasonable answers to problems 2 and 3?

LEARNING OBJECTIVE

Students check for hidden assumptions and change their points of view, if necessary, to solve nonroutine problems.

GROUPING

Individuals or pairs

MATERIALS

✳ *Think Again!* reproducible (p. 27)

ANSWERS

1. See page 64.
2. Sample answers: The egg is caught after it falls 15 feet, but before it hits the ground; it lands in water; it's hard boiled; it lands in something very soft, like cotton or sand.
3. Sample answers: Skier hits the tree, and the skis go past on their own; two people each ski on one ski; one ski is sent down, then another; skier stops at tree, steps off skis, walks around the tree while the skis slide by the tree, and then puts them on again on the other side of the tree in the same tracks; tree is small, and skier skis right over it; tree is pliant, and skier bends it as he or she passes by.

Think Again!

Solve these puzzlers. If these brain teasers seem
unsolvable at first, think again! Good luck!

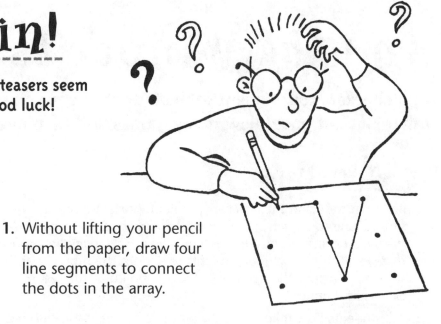

1. Without lifting your pencil
from the paper, draw four
line segments to connect
the dots in the array.

2. An egg dropped from a height of 15 feet does not break.
How is this possible?

_____

_____

_____

_____

_____

3. You see two parallel ski tracks coming down a snowy slope. At
one point, the tracks separate to go around a tree: one track
goes around to the left and the other track goes around to
the right. Then the tracks come together again and continue
on, side by side, down the slope. What might have caused
this peculiar sight?

_____

_____

_____

_____

_____

And the Winner Is...

In a checkers tournament each student in your class will play every other student once. How many games will be played in all?

➔ Directions

1. Before introducing the checkers problem, present a similar but simpler one to students: *A club has 4 members. Each member shakes the hand of each of the other club members. How many handshakes are there in all?* [6] Select four students to act out the problem and one student to record the handshakes on the board as the rest of the class calls them out.

2. Ask students how many handshakes there will be if the club has 6 members. Besides acting out the problem, what other strategies could they use to solve the problem? Give students a few minutes to solve it. Then discuss strategies and solutions. Make sure to talk about the following approaches:

   a. Use a geometric model: Make 6 dots in a circle. Connect each dot to each of the other dots. Count the number of line segments.

   b. Use number sense: All 6 people shake 5 others' hands, but since when A is shaking B's hand, B is shaking A's hand, there are half as many handshakes [$(6 \times 5) \times \frac{1}{2} = 15$].

3. Now present the checkers problem given below the title of the activity. Guide pairs to solve the problem in the most efficient manner. You might simplify the problem by asking for the number of games if only half the students in your class were playing. Encourage students to compare answers and methods.

☆ Taking It Farther

Tell students that in a single-elimination tournament, like the NCAA basketball championships, a team is out once it loses. Challenge them to figure out the number of games needed to determine the winner of a single-elimination chess tournament in which every student in your school participates. [One fewer than the number of students in the school, since all but one—the winner—must lose.]

✔ Assessing Skills

* Do students understand the solution methods presented?

* Are they able to explain how they obtained their answers to the checkers problem?

LEARNING OBJECTIVE

Students solve a problem by putting it into symbolic form.

GROUPING

Pairs

MATERIALS

None

Footsore

How long would it take to walk to Dallas?
Wait a minute—WALK?!

➜ Directions

1. Present the opening question to students; if your school is in or near Dallas, choose another, distant destination.

2. As preposterous as the proposition sounds, encourage students to work to find a reasonable response. Guide them along the way. For example, direct them to figure out how to determine average walking speed (time it by using a nearby quarter-mile running track, for instance) and what route to take to Dallas. Have them decide how realistic this walk would be and whether to factor in time for stopping at dark, eating, sleeping, getting tired from the exertion, sightseeing along the way, weather, and so on.

3. Have groups present their findings. They should tell their walking speed and how they determined it, describe their route and how they chose it, and give their predicted time of arrival in Dallas. Ask them to explain what was easiest, hardest, and most enjoyable about the investigation. Allow time for further discussion.

★ Taking It Farther

Give students the opportunity to figure out how long it would take them to complete another whimsical trip, such as a trip to Mars. Or challenge them to determine how long it would take them to count aloud to one million. Have them predict answers before starting.

✔ Assessing Skills

✳ Do students arrive at reasonable answers? Can they explain how they arrived at their answers?

✳ Do all group members participate actively in the investigation?

LEARNING OBJECTIVE

Students use proportional reasoning to solve a large problem by breaking it down into small steps.

GROUPING

Cooperative groups

MATERIALS

✳ watch or stopwatch
✳ road atlas

Preferred Seating

How can you arrange tables to seat the greatest number of people?

➛ Directions

1. Draw four squares side by side but not touching on the board. Ask students to imagine that they have four small square tables to arrange for a party. Tell them that each table seats one person at a side. Encourage students to find all the possible ways the tables can be arranged and how many people can be seated at each arrangement, and discuss their findings.

2. Duplicate and distribute a reproducible to each pair or group of students. Also pass out a sheet of graph paper to each student.

3. Have pairs or groups work through the seating problems presented on the reproducible. Tell students that they may describe their arrangements with multiplication sentences, drawings, or phrases. Make sure they understand the distinction between tables that touch completely along a side and those that do not. When students finish, discuss their answers as a whole-class activity.

4. Challenge students to share what they can generalize, for any number of square tables, about which table arrangements create the greatest number of seats [separate, individual tables] and which create the least number of seats [arrangement closest to a square].

5. Have students explain what they can conclude about the perimeters of rectangles that have the same area but different shapes. [The closer a rectangle is to a square shape, the smaller its perimeter.]

☆ Taking It Farther

* Have students imagine that they must seat twenty people using the same kind of small square tables. Tell them that the Be Seated Store rents these tables for $25 each. Let them figure out the least amount they can spend. [5 × $25 = $125]

* Challenge students to arrange the tables in the shape of their first names or initials. Have them record their work on graph paper.

✓ Assessing Skills

* Are students able to find the correct number of available seats in each arrangement?

* Can they state a relationship between the shape of the rectangle formed by the tables and the number of seats created?

LEARNING OBJECTIVE

Students investigate patterns to explore a relationship between area and perimeter.

GROUPING

Pairs or cooperative groups

MATERIALS

* *Preferred Seating* reproducible (p. 31)
* graph paper
* small squares, such as color tiles (optional)

ANSWERS

1. 48 people
2. 12 x 1: 26; 6 x 2: 16; 4 x 3: 14
3. Check students' drawings.
4. greatest number of people: 48; least number of people: 14

Preferred Seating

Everyone at the party will sit at twelve small square tables that you set up in the room, any way you choose. Each table seats one person on a side.

Answer the questions about possible seating arrangements. Use a table like the one below to record your answers.

ARRANGEMENTS FOR 12 TABLES

Description of Arrangement	Number of Seats

1. Suppose you arrange the tables so that none touch. How many people can you seat?

2. Make all the different rectangles you can using all 12 tables, for example, a 1 × 12 rectangle. How many people can you seat at each rectangle?

3. Make other arrangements of the tables. They can be irregular figures, but tables that are connected must touch completely along a side.

   Like this: ☐☐   Not like this: ☐☐

   How many people can sit at each arrangement?

4. What's the greatest number of people you can seat with your rectangular arrangements? What is the least number you can seat?

Is Jack a Millionaire?

We all know that not having money weighs on the mind. But do we know how much money actually weighs?

Directions

1. Bring in and/or have students bring in some quarters. Gather as many scales as you can from the school.

2. Tell students that Jack, a poor struggling artist, just won 10,000 pounds of quarters in a contest. (If your school has only metric scales available, change the amount to 4,500 kg of quarters.) Then ask, *Is Jack a millionaire?* Have students make their predictions.

3. Then guide them to answer this question using a wealth of critical thinking but an economy of money, time, and effort. Ask them to tell how many more pounds of quarters Jack would need if they find that 10,000 pounds isn't enough. [About 80 quarters weigh 1 lb; students may weigh a sixteenth (5 quarters), an eighth (10 quarters), or a quarter lb (20 quarters) to figure this out. They can use proportional reasoning to determine that about 50,000 lb of quarters equals $1 million. Poor Jack needs 40,000 more lb.]

4. Have students present their findings and explain the strategies they used to solve the problem. Compare methods. Ask students to tell which methods they think were most efficient.

Taking It Farther

Have students first predict, then figure out, how many pounds of either dimes, nickels, or pennies would make them millionaires.

Assessing Skills

* Are students able to find a reasonable answer to the problem? How do their answers compare with their initial guesses?

* How have they applied proportional reasoning to do so? Can they explain their reasoning?

LEARNING OBJECTIVE

Students apply proportional reasoning skills to solve a problem about weight and money.

GROUPING

Cooperative groups

MATERIALS

* postal scale or balance scale
* quarters (at least 10 per pair of students)

Toast French

Anyone can whip up some French toast—provided he or she knows the directions. Can students make French toast from a scrambled set of directions?

⟶ Directions

1. Tell students that it can be easy to prepare a meal when the steps are clearly written and listed in the right order. Then present the following steps for making French toast, pointing out that the steps are out of order. You might write the steps on the board and read them aloud for students to record or make a list and distribute copies of it.

2. Allow time for students to examine the list. Ask them to suggest steps left off the list such as shopping for bread or other ingredients, cleaning up, and so on. Then have them rearrange the steps into a sensible order. Explain to students that more than one order is possible. [Sample order: d, i, c, j, k, h, a, e, b, g, f]

The Steps

a. Melt butter in the frying pan.

b. Place the bread in the frying pan.

c. Crack the eggs into a bowl.

d. Collect the utensils you'll need: bowl, frying pan, fork, spatula.

e. Dip a piece of bread into the egg mixture.

f. Pour syrup over French toast.

g. Turn over bread when one side is browned.

h. Heat the frying pan.

i. Get the eggs from the refrigerator.

j. Beat the eggs.

k. Add sugar and cinnamon to eggs.

⭐ Taking It Farther

Let students use index cards to create their own set of scrambled directions for doing something. Classmates can unscramble them.

✔ Assessing Skills

✳ Are students able to place the steps in a sensible order?

✳ Are they able to explain the choices they made?

LEARNING OBJECTIVE

Students put the scrambled steps of a task into order.

GROUPING

Individual

MATERIALS

✳ index cards

On Madison Avenue

Jingle, jingle, who's got the jingle? Students put their heads together to create clever slogans for a variety of products.

⟲→ Directions

1. Provide one or two product slogans or jingles you think are effective. Ask students to share their favorite slogans or jingles. Brainstorm a list of others with your class. Discuss with students why they think these slogans are good ones.

2. Tell students that they'll get a chance to see if they have a future in advertising. As a group, they'll come up with some new, original, brilliant slogans that will make people run to buy some everyday products and services. Encourage them to be as creative or as funny as they can, but emphasize that the goal of the slogans is to sell products. Remind students to keep their market in mind.

3. Duplicate the *On Madison Avenue* reproducible and distribute one reproducible to each group.

4. Allow time for students to "pitch" their slogans to the rest of the class. Ask them to identify their market and explain why their creation will sell the product. Post their efforts on the bulletin board.

★ Taking It Farther

Invite students to create magazine, bus, or train ads for their products, in which they include artwork and designs along with their slogans.

✔ Assessing Skills

* Do students come up with slogans that match features of the products with interests of the people likely to buy them?

* Are they able to explain why they believe their slogans will be effective?

LEARNING OBJECTIVE

Students consider different products and the kinds of people who might buy them.

GROUPING

Cooperative groups

MATERIALS

✳ *On Madison Avenue* reproducible (p. 35)

On Madison Avenue

Look at the products listed below. Name and describe each.
Then put all your creative juices into coming up with clever
advertising slogans manufacturers would drool over.

Product	Name and Description	Slogan
sports car		
new magazine		
basketball sneaker		
new kind of sandwich		
cat food		
shampoo		
choose your own product		

Logically Speaking

Some events may or may not happen. See if students can describe the chances that an event will occur.

Directions

1. Present the following statement to students: *The sun will set tomorrow.* Ask if this event is "certain," "likely," "unlikely," or "impossible." Have students defend their responses. Then repeat the process for this statement: *You will listen to the radio this week.*

2. Tell students that they're going to read several statements. Then they will evaluate each one to determine the likelihood that it will occur.

3. Duplicate and distribute the *Logically Speaking* reproducible to each student. Depending on the ability level of your class, you might want to add "very likely" and "somewhat likely" to the list of possible answers.

4. Discuss students' answers. Encourage them to justify their responses, particularly when these differ from the answers most classmates give.

5. Then invite students to write and share statements they've formulated. Have others respond to them before asking for the answer the writer had in mind.

Taking It Farther

Create an interactive bulletin board based on this activity. Divide the space into six regions: *certain, very likely, likely, somewhat likely, unlikely, impossible.* Ask students to write statements on index cards and post them in the appropriate regions. Encourage them to read each other's statements and rearrange any they believe are misplaced.

Assessing Skills

✳ Do students understand the distinctions among the different descriptions?

✳ Are they able to make reasonable assessments of the likelihood of the events?

LEARNING OBJECTIVE

Students apply logical thinking, common sense, and an intuitive understanding of probability to describe the chances that an event will happen.

GROUPING

Individual

MATERIALS

✳ *Logically Speaking* reproducible (p. 37)

✳ index cards

Logically Speaking

What are the chances that you'll fly to Mars in your lifetime? No way, you say? But are you sure?

Describe the chances of each of the following events happening by choosing the best description from these choices: *certain, likely, unlikely, impossible.*

1. There will be oxygen in the air tomorrow. _____

2. It will snow sometime next week. _____

3. Someone in your class will be a senator one day. _____

4. Someone in your class will live in another country one day. _____

5. A giraffe will walk down your block this year. _____

6. You'll have homework this week. _____

7. There is life elsewhere in the universe. _____

8. Your favorite performer will appear in your area. _____

9. You'll get three heads if you flip a coin three times. _____

10. You'll see an eclipse this month. _____

11. You will eat a strange food this week. _____

Let's Be Reasonable

How well do students know American geography?
Well, do they know where the "middle of nowhere" is?

⟿ Directions

1. Tell students that although they may think they've been to the middle of nowhere, or even live there themselves, the people in one small American town know better—they *do* live there. Inform your young skeptics that every year, on the last weekend in June, the people of that town proudly hold a Middle of Nowhere Celebration.

2. Duplicate and distribute the *Let's Be Reasonable* reproducible to each student. Explain that their task is to think logically in order to make sensible guesses to complete statements about American geography. Good guesses will lead them to the middle of nowhere!

3. When students finish, you may want to have them discuss why some choices make sense and others do not. Refer them to an up-to-date almanac or other source to settle any geographical disagreements.

☆ Taking It Farther

Invite students to create their own "crack-the-code" activities that require applying critical thinking and common sense to geography or other social studies concepts.

✔ Assessing Skills

✳ Do students make reasonable guesses?
✳ Are they able to explain the logic they used to make their choices?

LEARNING OBJECTIVE

Students make reasonable guesses about geographic information.

GROUPING

Individual

MATERIALS

✳ *Let's Be Reasonable* reproducible (p. 39)
✳ United States almanac (optional)
✳ calculator (optional)

ANSWERS

1. W. 32 million
2. T. 480,000
3. N. 5,580
4. O. 282
5. E. 20,320
6. A. 1872
7. S. 1,545
8. H. 268,601
9. N. 1,932
10. R. 250,000
11. I. 65 million
Ainsworth, NE

Let's Be Reasonable

Just exactly where is the middle of nowhere?

To find out, first circle the best answer for each statement.
Then write the letter above the number in the code at the bottom.

1. California is the state with the largest population, about _____.
   V. 3,200   **W.** 32 million   **X.** 320 million

2. On the other hand, Wyoming has a population of about _____.
   T. 480,000   **U.** 48,000   **V.** 4,800

3. Alaska has the most coastline, about _____ mi.
   L. 558,000   **M.** 55,800   **N.** 5,580

4. The lowest point in the nation, Death Valley, is _____ ft below sea level.
   N. 0.282   **O.** 282   **P.** 2,820

5. The height of Mt. McKinley, the highest in the country, is _____ ft.
   D. 2,320   **E.** 20,320   **F.** 200,320

6. Yellowstone, the first national park, was founded in _____.
   A. 1872   **B.** 1802   **C.** 1772

7. The smallest state, Rhode Island, has an area of _____ sq mi.
   S. 1,545   **T.** 41,545   **U.** 241,545

8. Texas, the second largest, has an area of _____ sq mi.
   G. 86,861   **H.** 268,601   **I.** 6,168,601

9. Crater Lake, the deepest in the nation, is _____ ft deep.
   L. 32   **M.** 932   **N.** 1,932

10. Oklahoma has the largest Native American population, about _____.
    Q. 2,500   **R.** 250,000   **S.** 25 million

11. The number of Americans under age 18 is about _____.
    H. 1 million   **I.** 65 million   **J.** 200 million

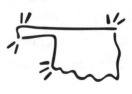

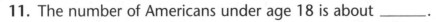

| 6 | 11 | 3 | 7 | 1 | 4 | 10 | 2 | 8 | 9 | 5 |

Under Cover

Sherlock Holmes excelled at gathering evidence that led to solutions. Cracking codes requires the same inferential thinking—but without the hat and pipe!

⟳→ Directions

1. Duplicate and distribute the *Under Cover* reproducible to each individual or pair.

2. Go over the directions with the class. Explain that each of the three codes uses a letter shift. This means, for example, A = B, B = C, C= D, and so on. Be sure students know that the code in each problem is different, and all numbers appear as written.

3. Guide students to look for clues. For instance, a single letter by itself is probably an *A* or *I*. A letter after an apostrophe is likely to be *S* or *T*. Some words appear often, such as *the*. Encourage students to test their hypotheses slowly.

4. You may want to provide hints for students to help them get started. Share as much or as little of the following information as you see fit:

   a. A = E, B = F, C = G, D = H, and so on.
   Or tell them that W = A and Z = D.

   b. A = Z, B = Y, C = X, D = W, and so on.
   Or tell them that Z = A and Y = B.

   c. A = O, B = P, C = Q, D = R, and so on.
   Or tell them that Z = N and Y = M.

5. Discuss solutions with the whole class. Encourage students to share their strategies.

☆ Taking It Farther

Have students make up their own codes based on letter shifting. They may use the codes to prepare secret messages for classmates to crack. Students who enjoy cracking codes may enjoy browsing through *Games* magazine or other sources to solve cryptogram puzzles.

✓ Assessing Skills

✳ What patterns or clues do students use to get started?

✳ Are they consistent in the way they crack codes?

✳ How do students go about creating their own codes?

LEARNING OBJECTIVE

Students attempt to crack codes to decipher secret messages. They also encode messages based on codes they devise.

GROUPING

Individuals or pairs

MATERIALS

✳ *Under Cover* reproducible (p. 41)

ANSWERS

1. in your eyes. They move more than 100,000 times a day.

2. the world's longest case of the hiccups. His hiccups lasted for 69.5 years!

3. the world's biggest seed. It can weigh as much as 44 pounds!

Under Cover

No, your eyes aren't playing tricks on you. Each statement starts out in plain English, then switches into code.

Each numbered problem below uses a different code, but all codes work by replacing one letter with another. Ask your teacher for a hint if you want one. Note: Numbers are not in code.

1. The most active muscles in your body are . . .

   mr csyv iciw. Xlic qszi qsvi xler 100,000 xmqjw e hec.

   _____

2. Poor Charles Osborne! He had . . .

   gsv dliow's olmtvhg xzhv lu gsv srxxfkh.

   _____

   Srh srxxfkh ozhgvw uli 69.5 bvzih!

   _____

3. What's so special about the double coconut? It has . . .

   hvs kcfzr'g pwuusgh gssr.

   _____

   Wh qob kswuv og aiqv og 44 dcibrg!

   _____

What Dwayne Likes

Sometimes it's hard to follow the logic in the decisions people make. Take Dwayne's "fan-fare," for example.

Directions

1. Explain to students that Dwayne is very particular about the sports teams he roots for. He roots for the Jets and Eagles but not the Giants or Steelers; he favors the Falcons over the Braves and the Hawks over the Pistons. Ask them to determine who Dwayne would root for in a game between the Rockets and the Bulls.

2. Discuss students' answers, allowing time for them to give their reasons. Point out (if someone has not already) that Dwayne roots only for teams named for things that fly. Then ask students to try to come up with other teams he would cheer for.

3. Now tell students that Dwayne is particular about other things too, such as what foods he'll eat, movies he'll see, or cities he'd like to live in. Duplicate and distribute the *What Dwayne Likes* reproducible to each group.

Taking It Farther

Challenge students to make up their own "What Dwayne Likes" problems and substitute their names and likes for Dwayne's. Encourage them to exchange problems and use logical reasoning to solve. Invite students to post the problems and solutions on the bulletin board or compile them in a "Class Likes" scrapbook.

Assessing Skills

* Do students use logical reasoning to identify attributes that link each group of items?

* Are they able to apply their understanding to answer the questions about Dwayne's preferences?

LEARNING OBJECTIVE

Students use logic to identify what items have in common.

GROUPING

Cooperative groups

MATERIALS

* *What Dwayne Likes* reproducible (p. 43)
* United States almanac

ANSWERS

1. Grapefruit; it ends with a consonant.
2. Tallahassee; it's a state capital.
3. Will Smith; his first name has only one syllable.
4. Taylor; he was born in Virginia.

What Dwayne Likes

Dwayne has an opinion about everything, but there's logic in his choices.

Read each statement about his preferences. Then try to think like Dwayne to answer each question.

1. Dwayne is a fussy eater. He'll eat corn, fish, meat, and carrots, but don't bother putting lettuce, tuna, or an apple on his plate. Which will he eat, pasta or grapefruit? Why?

_____

_____

_____

2. Dwayne is fussy also about the cities he'd live in. Phoenix, Hartford, Austin, and Sacramento make his list, but Los Angeles, Miami, Seattle, and Baltimore do not. Would he live in Tucson or Tallahassee? Why?

_____

_____

_____

3. Bruce Willis, John Wayne, Jim Carey, and Meg Ryan are are among Dwayne's movie stars; he'll see any movie they're in. On the other hand, no film with Harrison Ford, Julia Roberts, or Denzel Washington holds any interest for him. Which movie would he go to, one starring Will Smith, or one featuring Whoopi Goldberg? Why?

_____

_____

_____

4. Dwayne is partial to certain American presidents. George Washington, Thomas Jefferson, James Monroe, John Tyler, and Woodrow Wilson make his "A" list, but John Adams, Abraham Lincoln, Andrew Jackson, Richard Nixon, and Bill Clinton do not. Who makes Dwayne's list, Zachary Taylor or Ronald Reagan? Why? Hint: Look at a table with data about presidents.

_____

_____

_____

Chili Challenge

What's Mexican food without the chilies?

LEARNING OBJECTIVE

Students use logical reasoning or other strategies to solve a problem.

GROUPING

Individual or pairs

MATERIALS

None

◑▸Directions

1. Talk with students about the zesty flavors chilies add to dishes. Point out that there are many kinds of chilies, from the mild poblano to the hyper-hot habañero.

2. Then present the following problem for students to work on independently: *Imagine that 4 people line up for a chili taste test. In turn, one person after the next, they taste each of 5 different kinds of chilies: ancho, poblano, serrano, chipotle, and jalapeño. Each person takes 2 minutes at each tasting station—the chilies are hot, and tasters need time to hose down their taste buds! How long does it take all 4 people to pass through the line and complete the taste test?* [16 minutes]

3. Discuss students' strategies and solutions. Note that some will use logical reasoning. They can figure out that each of the 4 chili tasters needs 10 minutes to do the test—5 varieties of chilies for 2 minutes each. The last person in line has to wait for three people to finish tasting the first kind of chili—that's another 6 minutes, so the taste test takes 16 minutes.

4. Other students might make a table, such as the one started below, to solve the problem. Each number represents one of the 4 people.

	Ancho	Poblano	Serrano	Chipotle	Jalapeño
2 min	1				
4 min	2	1			
6 min	3	2	1		
8 min	4	3	2	1	
10 min		4	3	2	1

☆ Taking It Farther

Invite students to formulate problems—to solve by using logical reasoning, by making a table, or by another method—about people doing a series of tasks or waiting in lines.

✔ Assessing Skills

✳ Do students use an organized, logical approach to solve the problem?

✳ Do they use a combination of strategies?

All in a Family

You know the number of grandparents, parents, children, and grandchildren in a family. Do you know how many people are in the family?

⟹ Directions

1. Present the following problem: *In the Yu family, there are a grandmother and a grandfather. There are 3 mothers, 3 fathers, and 8 children (4 sisters and 4 brothers). There are 4 daughters and 4 sons and 1 daughter-in-law and 1 son-in-law. There are 3 grandsons and 2 granddaughters. What is the least number of people the Yu family could have?*

2. Guide students to work together to draw a tree diagram to solve the problem. Emphasize that they may need to try several diagrams but that they should use logical reasoning, for example, to decide where in the diagram to place the grandparents and grandchildren, and where the son-in-law and daughter-in-law must go. Remind students that they need to account for all information given in the problem and that their goal is to find the least number of people that could make up the family.

3. When discussing students' solutions, you might present the following family tree, which shows that the Yu family could have as few as 12 members.

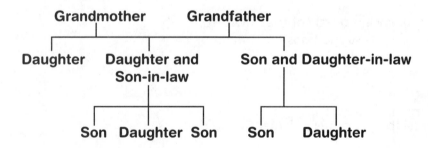

★ Taking It Farther

Invite students to use data about several generations of their own families to create tree-diagram problems like this for classmates to solve.

✔ Assessing Skills

✳ Have students found the least possible number of family members?
✳ Do their diagrams show all the information presented in the problem?

LEARNING OBJECTIVE

Students use a diagram and deductive logic to solve a problem.

GROUPING

Pairs

MATERIALS

None

Talent Show

Anyone in show business will tell you that performers can be picky. If entertainers don't get their way, the show's director may need to duck!

⟳→ Directions

1. Have students imagine that they're in charge of putting together a talent show of five fussy performing pets. Then present this list of all the pets' peeves:

   a. The hamster does headstands. He's a ham and wants to go last.

   b. The gerbil tells jokes. She's jumpy and won't go first.

   c. The puppy fetches. That's boring. Get this act over with early on.

   d. The kitten juggles yarn. She won't perform just before or after the dog or parakeet.

   e. The parakeet does funny impersonations. She won't follow a comic.

2. Duplicate, distribute, and discuss the *Talent Show* reproducible. Instruct students to complete the program for the pet talent show.

3. Have students compare their programs and discuss how they figured out a sequence of acts that meets all the performers' demands.

☆ Taking It Farther

Challenge students to formulate a sequencing puzzle of their own. You might brainstorm a list of topics and discuss suggestions for coming up with parameters.

✔ Assessing Skills

Do students' programs account for all the performers' demands and the time requirements?

LEARNING OBJECTIVE

Students use logical reasoning to place events in sequence.

GROUPING

Cooperative groups

MATERIALS

✳ *Talent Show* reproducible (p. 47)

ANSWERS

Possible order—puppy, parakeet, gerbil, kitten, hamster; times will vary.

Talent Show

Plan a schedule for a pet talent show by filling in the program below. Use the information given about your performers and this key requirement—all acts last about 15 minutes, no longer. (After all, how long would you want to listen to a gerbil's jokes?)

❋ Pet Talent Show ❋

Act	Time
Intermission for Pet Exercise and Water Break (20 minutes)	12 noon

Yechh!

Here's something you'll never hear a student say: "I'll have a liver and sauerkraut sandwich with hot peppers, and an order of lima beans, please."

➤ Directions

1. Tell students that a group of middle school students has been surveyed about their least favorite foods. The results show that 33 hate hot peppers, 30 hate liver, and 22 hate lima beans. Tell them that of this group of gourmets, 11 hate both hot peppers and lima beans, 15 hate both lima beans and liver, and 13 hate both liver and hot peppers. Tell them that 8 students hate all three foods. Then ask: *How many students were surveyed?* [54 students were surveyed; see Venn diagram at right.]

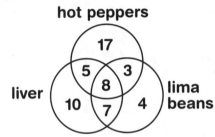

2. Elicit from students that answering the question is not simply a matter of adding 33, 30, and 22. Invite suggestions for approaches to use to find the answer. If students do not suggest it, point out the effectiveness of using a Venn diagram to show overlapping subsets.

3. As needed, review how to use a Venn diagram. Guide students to understand that intersections of any two regions represent the students who hate both those foods. Ask them to tell what the intersection of three regions represents. [those who hate all three foods] Ask them to tell how to use the diagram to find the total number of students surveyed. [Add the numbers.]

★ Taking It Farther

Have students survey friends about a topic of interest to them, such as a team they root for, a sport they play, a kind of music they enjoy, and so on. Emphasize that the answers must be limited to a few choices. Let students display their numerical results on the bulletin board but leave out the total number of people surveyed. Challenge other students to find out the number.

✓ Assessing Skills

✱ Have students used logical reasoning to find the relationship among data?

✱ Do they understand how to use a Venn diagram to show these relationships?

LEARNING OBJECTIVE
Students use a Venn diagram and logical reasoning to show relationships among data.

GROUPING
Individual or pairs

MATERIALS
None

One Step at a Time

The two multistep problems on this page might bring out students' best logical reasoning.

⟫ Directions

1. Present the following two problems for pairs or groups to work on:

   a. *You have six silver coins. Although they all look and feel exactly the same, one is a fake. It weighs less than the others. You also have a balance scale. How can you find the fake using only two weighings on your scale?*

   b. *You need to cook something for exactly 6 minutes. However, you have only a 5-minute timer and an 8-minute timer. How can you do it? How long will the whole process take?*

2. Provide ample time for students to try to solve these problems. If they have trouble getting started, encourage them to try more than one strategy. For example, they might act out the first problem and draw a diagram to solve the second. Then go over solutions and strategies. Acknowledge all successful approaches students use. Invite them to share their results with the rest of the class.

☆ Taking It Farther

Suggest that students try these puzzlers on family members. Also invite them to bring back any stumpers anyone at home knows.

✔ Assessing Skills

Do students attempt another strategy when one isn't working and they're stuck?

LEARNING OBJECTIVE

Students use logical reasoning to solve non-routine multi-step problems.

GROUPING

Pairs or small cooperative groups

MATERIALS

None

ANSWERS

Sample answers:

a. Place three coins on each pan, then weigh any two from the lighter pan; the fake is the lighter coin. If the pans balance, the fake is the coin not being weighed.

b. Start both timers; restart 5-minute timer when it goes off (2 minutes will be left on it when 8-minute timer goes off). Restart 8-minute timer when it goes off. Start the cooking when the 5-minute timer goes off again because there will be 6 minutes remaining on the 8-minute timer at that point. Total time: 5 minutes + 5 minutes + 6 minutes = 16 minutes.

49

To Tell the Truth

Like most people, you've probably experienced a situation much like the one described below.

Directions

1. Present the following sad situation:

   One huge piece of delicious apple pie was left after last night's feast. Mrs. Phibber was saving it for old Mrs. Kraemer next door. But, by morning, it was gone. One of the four Phibber children ate it. When Mrs. Phibber questioned them, these are the answers she got:

   Carl: *Toni ate it.*

   Toni: *Mike was the one who ate it.*

   Lizzie: *I didn't eat it.*

   Mike: *Toni lied when she said it was me.*

   If only one of the kids is telling the truth, who ate the pie?

2. Have students work together to try to figure out the truth. You might ask questions like these to help guide students' thinking:

   ✳ *Can Carl be the only one telling the truth? Why or why not?*

   ✳ *Can Toni be the only one telling the truth? Why or why not?*

   ✳ *So, who is telling the truth?* [Mike] *Who ate the piece of pie?* [Lizzie]

3. Ask students to explain their answers.

☆ Taking It Farther

Ask students to suppose that only one of the children was lying. Ask them to figure who was doing the lying and who ate the pie. [Toni, Toni]

✓ Assessing Skills

Are students able to reason logically to figure out who is and isn't telling the truth and who the guilty party is?

LEARNING OBJECTIVE

Students use logical reasoning to interpret the accuracy of statements people make.

GROUPING

Pairs or small cooperative groups

MATERIALS

None

Survey Savvy

Taking a survey can be an effective way of gathering data about a population—but it's important for the researcher to interpret the results accurately.

◦→ Directions

1. Ask students if they've ever participated in a survey. Spend a few minutes having them share their experiences. Then lead a discussion of the kinds of things that can affect the usefulness of survey results. Discuss, for example, how to evaluate the results of a survey about parallel parking skills based on the responses of seventh graders. Since these students don't drive yet, their responses would not represent drivers in general.

2. Now present the following survey topics and locations. Ask students to tell whether each location is appropriate for the survey. If they don't think it is, ask them to suggest another place or another topic. Invite discussion of students' suggestions, which are likely to vary.

Survey Topic	Location	Appropriate?	Reasons
favorite sport	ice hockey arena	[no]	[Reasons will vary.]
favorite comic book	comic-book convention	[yes]	[Reasons will vary.]
favorite actor	in a movie theater	[maybe]	[Reasons will vary.]
best pet	apartment building	[no]	[Reasons will vary.]

☆ Taking It Farther

Invite students to come up with their own matched and mismatched sets of survey topics and locations. Or challenge them to come up with both weak and strong survey questions to ask about topics of interest to them. Have them discuss why each question will or won't provide useful answers for the researcher.

✔ Assessing Skills

✳ Do students grasp why it's important to choose the right place for a survey?

✳ Can they explain why each location is or isn't an appropriate one?

LEARNING OBJECTIVE
Students use common sense to determine whether a location for a survey is one that can yield useful results.

GROUPING
Individual or pairs

MATERIALS
None

Muscular Matrix

You can use logic to solve many problems. One way is to organize data in a table and then use that table to eliminate possibilities.

➤ Directions

1. Duplicate and distribute the *Muscular Matrix* reproducible. Have students read the first problem. Point out that one way to solve a problem like this is to make a matrix. Then provide and discuss the following steps:

   ✳ Read all the clues to write the names and categories in the matrix.

   ✳ Find all clues with a definite yes or no. Mark Y or N in the appropriate boxes. Use this information to fill in other boxes in the same row or column. For instance, when you know which person runs track, you also know which ones don't.

   ✳ Go over each clue carefully, relating it to the other clues. Fill in the boxes with Ys or Ns until the problem is solved.

2. Draw this matrix for Problem 1 on the chalkboard or overhead projector:

	Jo	Vic	Kim	Brett	Juan
Track					
Soccer					
Baseball					
Swimming					
Water Polo					

3. As students present their answers, ask them how they used logic to eliminate possibilities.

☆ Taking It Farther

Have groups create their own matrix logic problems for classmates to solve. Help them make sure their clues give enough, but not too much, information.

✓ Assessing Skills

✳ Are students able to set up their tables correctly?

✳ Do they use clues to eliminate possibilities and identify the correct answers?

Muscular Matrix

Use a matrix to solve each problem.

1. Jo, Vic, Kim, Brett, and Juan tried out for different high school sports teams. The teams are track, soccer, swimming, baseball, and water polo. Use the clues to match each student with the team he or she tried to make.

CLUES

a. Jo didn't try out for any water sports because she never learned to swim.

b. Juan doesn't like ball sports, but he has found a sport he does enjoy.

c. Kim and Vic watched the swimming, track, and soccer teams work out, but neither tried out for those teams.

d. Kim, Jo, and Brett rarely see their pal, who's at baseball practice after school most days.

e. Brett made the swimming team.

2. Use the following clues to determine how the teams in the Central Division of the National Football League placed in 1995. Put that almanac away!

CLUES

a. Only one team finished behind Minnesota.

b. Detroit finished ahead of Tampa Bay.

c. Chicago finished behind Green Bay.

d. Chicago did not come in last.

e. Detroit did not win the division.

f. More than one team finished ahead of Chicago.

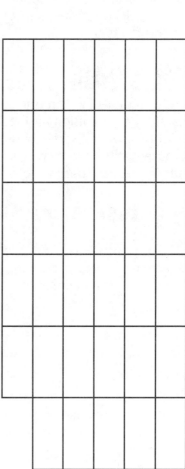

Is That So?

Do students believe everything they read? If so, lots of advertisers would like to know them better.

⟿ Directions

1. Talk with students about how reading ads carefully and thoughtfully helps them to be wiser consumers.

2. Present the following ad: *Twenty-five of the teens we asked preferred new Shimmer Shampoo.* Ask students to brainstorm a list of questions they'd want to have answered before they purchased this product. Students might ask, among other things: *To what did they prefer Shimmer—peanut butter? How many teens were asked—suppose 4,000 were? How were the teens chosen? Of those they asked, how many actually answered?* Have students come up with as many questions as they can about the vague claims this ad makes.

3. Duplicate and distribute the *Is That So?* reproducible to each student or pair. Then ask them to share the questions they have about the products.

★ Taking It Farther

Have students flip through magazines and newspapers and listen carefully to television and radio commercials. Ask them to think critically about the advertisers' claims and identify any that are misleading or that arouse healthy skepticism. Invite students to post or summarize these iffy ads in the classroom for others to examine.

✔ Assessing Skills

✳ Do students notice what may be misleading about the ads?

✳ Are they able to come up with reasonable questions the ads leave unanswered?

LEARNING OBJECTIVE

Students use logical reasoning to interpret information in advertisements.

GROUPING

Individual or pairs

MATERIALS

✳ *Is That So?* reproducible (p. 55)

ANSWERS

Sample answers:

1. How many were interviewed? At what is BRITE toothpaste #1? What difference does it make that people said it was #1?

2. Who says it's delicious? How much juice does it contain?

3. What kind of research is involved, and does it have anything to do with cereal?

4. Who cares what it looks like? How do you know what a dog thinks, or whether it agrees with you?

Is That So?

Read the ads on this page. Decide what information is missing or misleading.
Write questions you'd want to have answered before you'd buy the product.

1.

"90% of the people we interviewed said that BRITE toothpaste is #1."

_____
_____
_____
_____
_____

2.

"Thousands of Americans start their day with a full glass of delicious PEPPY PUNCH, which has real fruit juice in it."

_____
_____
_____
_____
_____

3.

"I'm involved in research. SPUDBUD is the best-tasting cereal. You should go out and buy a box right now."

_____
_____
_____
_____
_____

4.

"Bowser and I agree—no other dog food looks better in a bowl than Bit-o-Meat."

_____
_____
_____
_____
_____

Graphs Under Fire

Sometimes there's more than meets the eye in the way a graph is constructed. The visual impression a graph creates may not match the data it presents.

⟶ Directions

1. Discuss with students that, like words, graphs can be misleading and even purposely deceptive. Elicit from them ways that graph makers can present accurate data in ways that are visually misleading. If it is not suggested, point out that changes in the vertical or horizontal scales can change the impression a graph gives. As an example, sketch the following graph on the chalkboard or overhead projector and talk about how it presents accurate data in a misleading way.

PRICES RISE GRADUALLY

2. Guide students to recognize that although the line in the graph rises gradually, the increase in price is dramatic—it doubles in 5 months.

3. Duplicate and distribute the *Graphs Under Fire* reproducible to each student or pair. Provide time for students to discuss their evaluations.

☆ Taking It Farther

Challenge students to construct two graphs, both showing the same data, but each giving a different visual impression of that data.

✔ Assessing Skills

✳ Can students identify what is misleading about each graph?

✳ Do they see that it's how the graph is constructed, not the data, that is misleading? Can they convey the reason for the impression the graph gives?

LEARNING OBJECTIVE

Students examine graphs to identify what is misleading about them.

GROUPING

Individual or pairs

MATERIALS

✳ *Graphs Under Fire* reproducible (p. 57)

✳ overhead projector (optional)

Graphs Under Fire

Examine each graph below. Tell why it is misleading.

1.

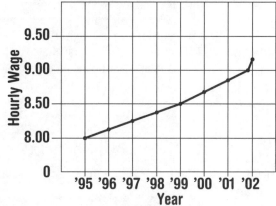

Factory Wages Rise Dramatically

_____
_____
_____
_____
_____
_____
_____

2.

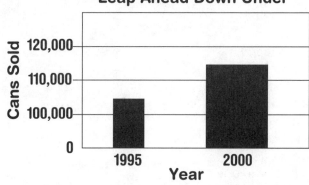

**Kangaroo Food Sales
Leap Ahead Down Under**

_____
_____
_____
_____
_____
_____
_____

3.

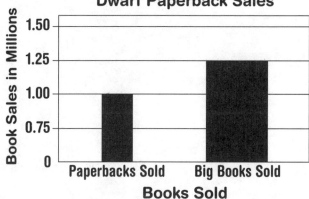

**Big Book Sales
Dwarf Paperback Sales**

_____
_____
_____
_____
_____
_____
_____

Getting Across

Here is a new twist on two old standbys.

⟳→ Directions

1. Present this problem to students, telling them to solve it any way they can:

   Calvin is on one side of a river with his collie, his cat, and his canary. He wants to bring all three across in a small boat. However, Calvin can take only one of them with him in the boat at a time. In addition, he can't leave the collie alone with the cat or the cat alone with the canary. Explain how Calvin can get all his pets across the river in one piece. [Sample answer: Bring cat across, come back and bring the dog across, returning with the cat. Leaving the cat, bring the canary across. Then come back and get the cat a second time.]

2. Help students who are stuck by suggesting that they decide which pets can be left alone together. Then invite volunteers to give their answers and share the strategies they used.

3. When students are at the height of their problem-solving powers, present this stumper:

   Ted, Lisa, and their mother and father had to get from an island to shore. However, their raft could safely hold only up to 215 pounds. Ted weighs 95 pounds; Lisa, 80 pounds; mom, 140 pounds; and dad, 180 pounds. Somehow they made it across. How did they do it? [Sample answer: Ted and Lisa crossed, then one returned with the boat. Dad crossed alone and the other child brought the boat back. Both children recrossed and then one of them brought the boat back for mom. Mom crossed alone. The child on shore went back for the one still on the island. Both children crossed back to shore together.]

4. Have volunteers explain how they obtained answers.

☆ Taking It Farther

Post any puzzling problems students know, perhaps some they've learned from family members or friends. Leave these up for classmates to work on in their spare time.

✔ Assessing Skills

✳ How did students apply logical reasoning to solve the problems?

✳ What problem-solving strategies did they use?

Students use logical reasoning and one of several strategies to solve nonroutine problems.

Pairs or small groups

None

Do I Have Problems!

Incorporate these Problems of the Day into your math curriculum daily or weekly. You may want to copy the problems on the board or on construction paper and then post them on a bulletin board or in your Math Center. To build auditory skills, you can also read aloud the problems to students.

MAGIC MARBLES

You have 50 red marbles, 50 white marbles, and 50 blue marbles. You have four identical jars. How would you distribute all the marbles into the jars so that if you were blindfolded and the jars were rearranged, you'd have the best chance of reaching into one jar and choosing a red marble? [Sample answer: Put 1 red marble in each of three jars; put all remaining 147 marbles in the fourth jar.]

BOWL THEM OVER

Suppose that 10 bowling pins were set up backward—4 in the front row, 3 in the next row, and so on. How could you reset them correctly by moving exactly 3 pins? [See drawing below.]

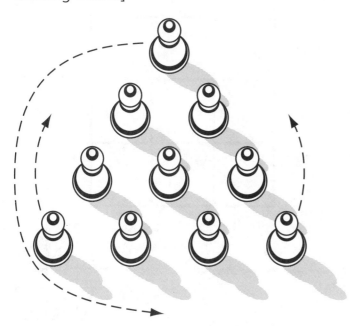

STAMP STUMPER

Jermaine spent $2.20 on letter stamps and postcard stamps. Letter stamps cost $0.32 and postcard stamps cost $0.20. How many of each did he buy? [5 letter stamps, 3 postcard stamps]

AN AGE-OLD QUESTION

The sum of the ages of the three Perez sisters is 50. Rosa is the youngest, Elena is the middle sister, and Felicia is the oldest—10 years older than Rosa. Five years ago, their ages were prime numbers. How old was each then? [7, 11, and 17]

PENNIES FOR A PENCIL?

A pen and a pencil together cost $5.10. The pen costs $5 more than the pencil. How much does each cost? [pen, $5.05; pencil $0.05]

BE REASONABLE

Use the numbers 45, 4, and 184 to fill in the blanks in a way that is reasonable. Then answer the question.

All _____ students in the grade are going by bus to the play. Will _____ buses be enough if each can hold _____ students?

[184, 4, 45; no]

WHO'S YOUNGER?

Anna is younger than Billy, and older and shorter than Carl. Billy is younger and taller than Diane. Diane is taller than Carl. Of the four, who is the oldest, the youngest, the tallest, and the shortest? [oldest: Diane; youngest: Carl; tallest: Billy; shortest: Anna]

WHAT'S THE POINT?

In the basketball league Ivy belongs to, 2 points are awarded for every shot made and 3 points are deducted for every shot missed. In one game, Ivy took 40 shots but scored 0 points. How many shots did she make? How many did she miss? [24 shots made, 16 shots missed]

A GOOD DAY'S WORK

Ed bakes and sells cookies. He earned $15 in 6 days, each day earning $0.50 more than on the previous day. How much did Ed earn on the first day? [$1.25]

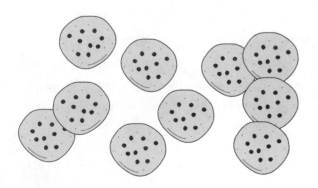

OUTFIELD OR INFIELD?

Every player on Ellen's baseball team can play the infield or the outfield. Ten can play the outfield positions only. Thirteen players can only play the infield. Six can play both the infield and the outfield positions. How many players can play the outfield positions? How many can play the infield positions? How many are on the team? Draw a Venn diagram. [outfield: 16; infield: 19; 29 on the team; see Venn diagram below]

infield   outfield

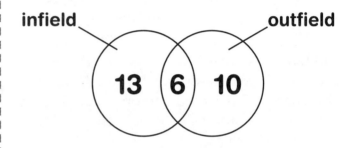

SEEING STARS

You may place only one star in each small square in the grid below. What is the greatest number of stars you can place without ever getting three in a row horizontally, vertically, or diagonally? [6 stars; see diagram below]

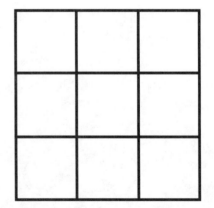

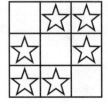

SPREAD THE WORD

Matty called Hattie with the big news. Then Hattie called 3 other people to tell them. Each of these people called 3 other people. Then each of them called 3 other people, each of whom called 3 other people. If all the callers spread the big news, how many people heard what Matty told Hattie? [121, including Hattie: 1 + 3 + 9 + 27 + 81 = 121]

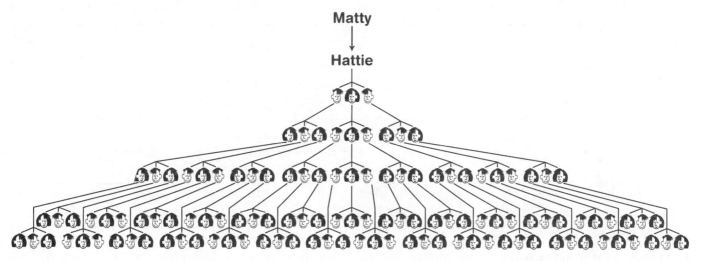

TIME TO PRACTICE

Five musicians from TOAN-DEF met to rehearse. They arrived at 10-minute intervals. None came at the same time. Andre was the last to arrive, at 10:00. Kent wasn't the first to get there. Reba arrived between the times that Kent and Karl did. Suki arrived 30 minutes before Karl. What time did each musician arrive at the rehearsal? [Suki, 9:20; Kent, 9:30; Reba, 9:40; Karl, 9:50; Andre, 10:00]

TIME FLIES

Luisa noticed that in 7 years she'll be half her mother's age. If, 3 years ago, Luisa was $\frac{1}{3}$ her mother's age, how old is her mother now? [33]

WORKING TOGETHER

Kevin can do a job in 4 hours. It takes Kendra 2 hours to do the same job. If they do the job together, how long will it take them? [1$\frac{1}{3}$ hours]

FISHING FOR ANSWERS

A fast-food chain is considering adding a tuna burger to its menu. Write a question (or questions) for a survey designed to learn how customers would react to this new product. Try to make your questions as useful to the chain as possible. [Questions will vary but should provide for a range of very specific answers.]

TIME TO LAUGH

At a convention of comics, there were jokesters (J), pranksters (P), and cut-ups (C). Seventy jokesters were in attendance, and there were:

20 who were both C and J but not P.

20 who were C but neither J nor P.

15 who were both C and P but not J.

35 who were P but neither C nor J.

20 who were J and P but not C.

30 who were J but neither P nor C.

How many comics made the audience laugh for more than 15 seconds? [Who knows?!]

In My Opinion

The activity _____ was:

Easy   Hard

because:

_____

_____

_____

_____

My work on this activity was:

poor   fair   good   excellent

because:

_____

_____

_____

I used the following math strategy or strategies:

◎→ _____   ◎→ _____

◎→ _____   ◎→ _____

◎→ _____   ◎→ _____

I would share this tip with someone who is about to do this activity:

_____

_____

_____

Student

UNDERSTANDING					
Identifies the problem or task.					
Understands the math concept.					
SOLVING					
Develops and carries out a plan.					
Uses strategies, models, and tools effectively.					
DECIDING					
Is able to convey reasoning behind decision making.					
Understands why approach did or didn't work.					
LEARNING					
Comments on solution.					
Connects solution to other math or real-world applications.					
Makes general rule about solution or extends it to a more complicated problem.					
COMMUNICATING					
Understands and uses mathematical language effectively.					
COLLABORATING					
Participates by sharing ideas with partner or group members.					
Listens to partner or other group members.					
ACCOMPLISHING					
Shows progress in problem solving.					
Undertakes difficult tasks and perseveres in solving them.					
Is confident of mathematical abilities.					

SCORING RUBRIC

3	2	1
Fully accomplishes the task.	Partially accomplishes the task.	Does not accomplish the task.
Shows full understanding of key mathematical idea(s).	Shows partial understanding of key mathematical idea(s).	Shows little or no grasp of key mathematical idea(s).
Communicates thinking clearly using oral explanation or written, symbolic, or visual means.	Oral or written explanation partially communicates thinking, but is incomplete, misdirected, or not clearly presented.	Recorded work or oral explanation is fragmented and not understandable.

ANSWERS

page 20: Following Directions

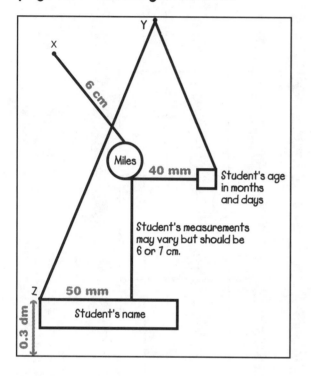

page 27: Think Again!

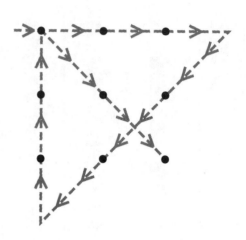

pages 23: Mapmaker, Mapmaker

Sample answers:

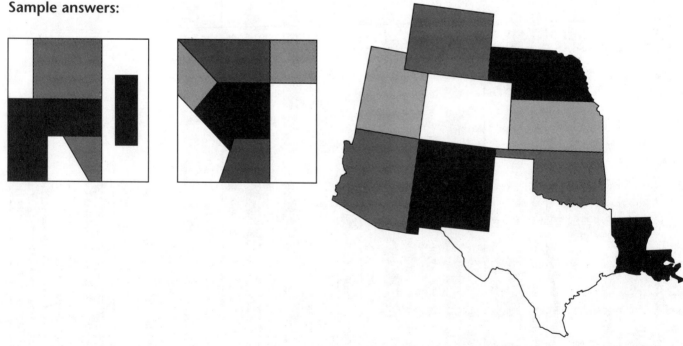